The Monster Who Killed
His Family Twice

The Monster Who Killed His Family Twice

THE TRUE STORY OF THE DEARBORN HEIGHTS MURDERS

BY FAITH BROWN

StoryTerrace

To my children: Chadney Jr., Kara, Koi, and Kaleigh.
You all brought me so much love and joy.

Text Michelle Booth, on behalf of StoryTerrace
Design StoryTerrace
Copyright © Faith Brown

First print August 2022

StoryTerrace

www.StoryTerrace.com

CONTENTS

1. IT WAS DESTINED — 7
2. BELIEVING IN MYSELF — 15
3. BECOMING A MOTHER — 23
4. DEVIL IN DISGUISE — 31
5. TORMENT — 37
6. ONE MORE YEAR — 49
7. THE TRAGEDY — 55
8. ANSWERS AND QUESTIONS — 61
9. STARTING OVER — 71
EPILOGUE — 81
RESOURCES — 113

1
IT WAS DESTINED

God, please send somebody, I prayed. *Wake my mom up, or somebody. Anybody . . . send somebody to help us.* I was desperate. I thought he was going to kidnap my two youngest daughters. I never thought he was going to kill anyone.

I was lying on the floor in the basement next to my son Chadney and my oldest daughter, Kara. Each of our mouths, wrists, knees, and ankles were duct-taped and we were being held at gunpoint by my husband at the time.

He was wearing a baseball cap like he was getting ready to go somewhere. He was sitting on top of a counter with his legs hanging over the front edge and his feet dangling in front of him. I can't recall a lot of what he was saying—a result of the trauma from that night—but I do remember he just kept talking and talking and talking. It was not like what you see in the movies where the guy holding the gun is yelling and frantic and beating his captives. My husband was not angry. He was calm and spoke in a normal tone as though he was having a regular conversation with us. There was just a little anxiety in his voice.

He was talking so much that there were times when I was not even listening to him. Instead my mind was racing to come up with a way to get my kids out of danger.

I could tell when I came home from work earlier that day that my husband was in one of his moods—upset about something but unwilling to communicate with me. I had gotten used to his mood swings and by this point in our relationship I had given up trying to talk to him when he acted this way. My goal in the past few weeks had become finding a new place for me and my children to live.

I had left my husband once before in 2013. We lived apart for several years before deciding to get back together again. He made me believe that he had changed, and things were different for a while, but after a few months I started seeing the same behavior patterns. I saw how he was disrupting our entire household and I saw how nervous my kids were. *I can't do this again*, I thought. *I need to get out of this and get my kids counseling.* There was no way for me to stay and help my husband to be better and prosper and I knew I could not try to regroup and build a new life by staying in a situation that was so messed up. I just wanted to get out and stay out for good. My kids and I were ready to move on and start a new life.

My husband knew I was going to divorce him. I had talked to him about it and told him the reasons why. He got that mad look in his eyes and asked me where the divorce papers were; I told them I didn't have them yet but that they would be coming soon. He wanted to try counseling, but he had said this a few years ago and we never went. I was willing back then but this time I told him no. It was clear that he hadn't changed, and now it was too late. I knew it was never going to work.

The process server came to our house on a Saturday in August 2016. Chadney answered the door and told my husband there was someone there to see him. My husband went to the door, took the papers, threw them down, and immediately started yelling and cussing. The process server asked to see me; he said he had never served anyone where the couple was still in the same household, and it made him uneasy. He gave me his card and asked me to keep in touch with him and I told him I would. My husband continued yelling for the next twenty minutes and started getting ready for work. He finally left and I went to sleep. I called the process server a little while later to let him know that I was okay, and I called him a few more times over the next several weeks.

My husband got really weird after that day. When I would come home from work, he would leave. If I cooked dinner, he would not eat it. If he was off work, he would leave the house and not come home until hours later. I never knew where he went or what he was doing. He would not speak to me unless it had something to do with Koi and Kaleigh and their school. It was the start of a new school year. Koi was in first grade; Kaleigh had just turned four and was in Head Start. Otherwise, there was no verbal communication at all from my husband. We had one conversation about a school field trip, which he said I would have to pay for, and he stopped paying for anything for Koi and Kaleigh after that. We lived like this for several more weeks. I had started looking for a new place to live and I was hoping to find something in the next week or two. I never got the chance.

It was during this time that my husband started parking his car in a different spot, closer to the house. That was unusual, but I knew if I asked him about it, he would either refuse to talk to me or it would turn into an argument. I was so tired of fighting with him and all I wanted to do was get out of there so I just let it go.

When I pulled into the driveway after work on September 20, 2016 I noticed something else unusual, that my husband had cleaned the carport and the garage. We had been arguing about it for a while. He wanted me to do it for some reason, but I was not going to work all day and then come home to clean them all by myself. I said I would do it the next time Kara or Chadney were home and could help me. So when I came home that day and saw my husband had cleaned them, I thought it was a little strange. I asked him where he had put a few things, but he still would not speak to me.

I finally gave up and went inside the house to spend time

with Koi and Kaleigh and feed them dinner. A few hours later, I gave them their baths and put them to bed. Then I left to pick Kara up from work and bring her back home. I could tell my husband was still in a bad mood when we walked in the house. He looked at me from where he was sitting on the couch and said, "You know you fucked up, right?" I just ignored him because I knew he would be waking me up to fight about it later that night.

That was something else I had gotten used to. Throughout our marriage, my husband would often spend all evening in a bad mood about something. I would try to talk to him about it and help him, but he would just sit there, staring straight ahead, not saying a word. I would eventually give up and go to bed. A few hours later he would wake me up saying he wanted to talk about something. Most of the time he wanted to argue, sometimes for hours. This cycle happened so often that I could tell when it was coming. This was one of those nights.

I went to bed at around 10:30 p.m. and the next thing I knew he was waking me up. I had only been asleep for about an hour when he came into the bedroom and said, "Hey, you need to get up." All I could think was, *What do you want? Ugh, you are getting on my nerves right now. I'm trying to sleep.* There was no way he was going to let me go back to sleep so I mentally prepared myself for another long night of arguing. I followed him to the living room and saw Chadney sitting on the couch. I could tell Chadney was sleepy and I thought, *You woke my son up, too?* My husband said he wanted to talk to us about something so I sat down next to Chadney.

Then the tragedy began.

As I watched the story unfold on television from my hospital bed hours later, I heard several inaccuracies being reported about me and my family. But I was also learning important bits of information I hadn't known before. It was like missing pieces of a puzzle were finally fitting into place. Things that I had not been able to understand about my husband all these years were starting to become clear.

It was in the hospital when I learned the truth about what happened to my husband's first wife—from the media, just like everyone else. That was also when I learned that my father had written letters to the parole board in support of my husband's early release from prison. I was in shock. Confused. I did not know what to think and I was certainly not capable of processing it all at the time.

I later learned that my husband had a plan to harm me all along. In his words during his interrogation, what he did to me "was destined." That messed me up even more to know that someone I loved and had kids with had it out for me. He had planned to do what he did. I was devastated.

I am not the same person I was before September 21, 2016. I never will be. It is impossible after going through a tragedy like that. That person no longer exists. Moving forward has not been easy. I have physical scars and I also suffer from depression, post-traumatic stress disorder, and short-term memory loss. But as I read in my statement at my husband's sentencing, I will not suffer like he intended for me to do. What he tried to do didn't work. My husband did not break me.

I am writing this book because I want to set the record straight about the things that were misreported about me and my family in the media. But more important, I want to share my experience as a survivor of domestic violence so it can help other people—women and men—who are in similar situations.

There are people who have read articles or seen stories in the news or watched videos about my tragedy that have been quick to judge me. There will be people who read this book that will do the same. They do not understand the decisions I made. How could I marry someone who was in prison for killing his first wife and unborn child? How could I move back in with him after being separated for two years? How could I have stayed with him so long in the first place? The reason people do not understand is because they have never been in a domestic violence situation. That is a blessing for them, but it also means they can't relate to what I have been through. You can't judge someone else's life by your background. You don't know how they grew up or what their experiences were. You have not walked in their shoes, and you have not walked in mine.

Shouldn't the real questions be, how was my husband granted parole in the first place? How was justice served there? Who failed him as a kid? Who knew he was a violent person and did nothing? And why did he take six innocent lives—four of them my children? The only person to blame for this violence and death is my husband.

If I could go back, there are things I would have done differently. I know I did the best I could at the time, but I wish I would have known the signs. I wish I would have known what to do. I watched my mother and father deal with their marital issues, sometimes not in the best way. So when my husband and I started to have issues of our own, I had no idea how to handle it.

It was not okay for my husband to treat me the way he did. I did not know what the red flags were to watch out for in a relationship, and I had seen some of those red flags in my own household when I was growing up, so they were not unusual to me. It is my hope to help educate people so they understand what to look out for, when it is time to seek help, and where they can go for help if they are in a domestic violence situation.

This is my story of survival.

2

BELIEVING IN MYSELF

The first time I saw my future husband I was fourteen years old. It was on a Sunday in 1991 and we were attending the same service at my dad's church, Church of the Risen Christ. I thought he was really cute. I had a crush on him, but he had no idea how I felt. We never officially met or even spoke back then. I just admired him from afar.

He was at church for a while and then he wasn't. I didn't think much about it. I had just started high school and I was enjoying spending time with my friends and doing all the things kids that age do.

I would not see him again for seventeen years.

———

My dad has been a pastor for over thirty years but he does not hide the fact that he had trouble in his past. He was incarcerated for civil rights disturbances and activism when he lived in Connecticut in the sixties and seventies, a time when black people were protesting and advocating for fairness and justice. Later, he battled with drug and alcohol addiction for several years, but he found his way into treatment and did the work to get himself clean and keep his family together.

I don't know exactly how it happened—I was only a baby at the time—but my dad heard about Adult & Teen Challenge, a faith-based recovery program in Detroit, Michigan. He was in treatment there for a while and then in 1978, my mom, my older brother Elijah, and I moved there to live with him. It was a residential program and back then the families of the recovering addict were allowed to live there, too.

We lived on the campus for about a year and then after my dad finished the program, we moved into our first house in Michigan. Then he started working at Christian Guidance Center as a counselor where he nurtured and mentored other men in treatment for addiction and became a spiritual mentor to many of them. That work led to him becoming a pastor and starting a church.

My dad has often admitted from the pulpit that he made mistakes when he was younger. Because of his past and his personal struggle with addiction, he has a heart for people who have been incarcerated. He has lived in that world and knows what it's like and understands what they go through. He wanted to do what he could to support them as they tried to start over and rebuild their lives. Many of the men he worked with and mentored through the recovery program joined Church of the Risen Christ, and formerly incarcerated individuals did, too. He welcomed them with open arms.

I liked going to church when I was very young. The churches we went to were fun. They engaged you and it made you want to learn about God. It was all in the way that they taught. It felt positive and inviting. It was a very different situation for me at home.

My dad was very strict with us, especially when it came to church. He would make us get up and pray every morning and go to church several days a week. Eventually we started having Bible study at our home. Once my dad became a pastor it was even worse. Then he would make us go to church six or seven days a week, and for a while that was our life. By that point I did not like going to church anymore. It felt forced upon us, not welcoming. I believe there should have been more of a balance.

Sometimes my dad was strict to the point that he didn't have patience with us; he wanted us to understand things right away. In first and second grade I had a really hard time with reading and task comprehension. He tried to help me with that a lot, he just went about it in the wrong way. I always had a fear of my dad. Even if he would call to me—whether I was in trouble with him or not—I would be so scared, holding my breath, afraid of what he would do next.

It was like those old wives' tales . . . instill the fear of God in your child. It wasn't like that all the time, but it was like that a lot of the time.

I was much more comfortable at home when my dad was not around. I could not relax with him there because I felt we weren't free to be kids. Sometimes kids do things. Sometimes they act up or make mistakes. I felt like there was extra pressure on us. When people came to our house we would tell them, "You can't do this . . . you can't do that . . ." It could be a little harsh at our house and it put us in an uneasy situation but there were a lot of rules and we had to follow them.

I had some good times with my dad, especially when he would play with us. He used to enjoy making things and I found that so intriguing. I would watch him as he worked, and he did not mind my curiosity. That was the only time I was not nervous or scared around him; he seemed more patient with us during those times.

Growing up, we were not allowed to listen to secular music or go to school dances. My dad made an exception one time and let us go to a dance. I felt so happy about that. On the weekends we were allowed to spend the night at someone's house, but we still had to go to church the next morning. We would have to go back home so we could attend church with my parents, but then they started letting us go to church with our friends.

Friends could spend the night at our house, and they

did sometimes, but I preferred to spend the night at their house. It was better that way. I felt more free and more relaxed, like it was okay to be myself. That was when I had the most fun—when I was able to get out of the house—to get away—and hang out with my friends.

I was a tomboy back then and I loved to play outside. We went to the park all the time and we rode our bikes a lot. It was a while before we were allowed to participate in extracurricular activities at school, but I loved when we could finally go to football games and other events because it meant I could spend more time with my friends.

―――――

Children need constant encouragement, and I did not have that when I was young. I was a fearful child and scared of the dark. There were a lot of times when I felt I was not good enough, and I did not have confidence like I should have when I was growing up—not until my senior year.

Seventh and eighth grades were a little challenging for me. I struggled with geometry in eighth grade and I would ask the teacher a lot of questions. I was not the only one. The teacher would tell us, "Nobody ask questions and don't come up to my desk." I would sit in that class and cry because I wanted to learn but I could not get the help I needed. I had such a hard time with geometry that I ended up having to go to summer school. I learned better there.

I had a different teacher and the way he broke the lessons down was easier for me to understand.

I had to take algebra in tenth grade and my teacher was the exact opposite of my geometry teacher. My algebra teacher was nice, and he encouraged his students. He always had something good to say to us. I had not experienced positive reinforcement like that before and it felt good.

I went to my teacher with a question one day and he was patient and kind and took the time to explain the answer in a way that I could comprehend it. I was about to walk back to my desk when he said one more thing to me that I will never forget. He told me I was not living up to my full potential. It was a pivotal moment in my life.

For the first time, I felt like someone believed in me. But more important, I started to believe in myself. A big reason for that was because of the way he was teaching me. He said, "If you have questions, ask." After that conversation I started really paying attention in class.

I had been scared to ask too many questions because of my geometry teacher, but my algebra teacher did not mind if I had ten million questions. He would even stay after school to help me when I needed it. I earned an A in algebra and I felt really good about that.

My confidence continued to grow during high school, once again with encouragement from my algebra teacher. I started jogging in tenth grade, partly to relieve the stress I was feeling from being at home, but I also liked the exercise.

At first I would jog around our neighborhood and at the park near our house. Eventually I started riding my bike to the high school and jogging there. My algebra teacher was also the boys' track coach, and he would notice me jogging around. He suggested I try out for cross country, so I did and I made the team.

I ran cross country my entire senior year. I felt good physically, but I also felt good about myself. There were positive changes at home, too. My dad started acting different toward me once I made the cross-country team. He came to a lot of my practices and all of my track meets and he would encourage me and the other girls on the team. It was the first time I had ever seen my dad interested in me and engaged like that. It was the first time I felt like he showed me love. It made me feel good.

3

BECOMING A MOTHER

I met my high school sweetheart in tenth grade. I was not allowed to have boys over or even receive phone calls from boys for a long time, so when I got caught talking to him on the phone my junior year, I was punished for it. But after that I was allowed to get calls from boys—although I still could not have boys over unless it was someone from church.

I would sneak out at night to see my boyfriend because my dad certainly was not going to let me date. I had a little more freedom after I graduated high school so my boyfriend and I would go on dates to the movies or dinner or bowling—and we had a lot of sex. I was in love.

My son, Chadney, was born August 7, 1997 and my first daughter, Kara, was born almost two years later on April 25, 1999. None of my pregnancies were bad, but my first one was the best. I had a few headaches and a little morning sickness in the beginning but then that passed. I could still do the things I liked to do. I walked all the time, rode my bike, jumped rope . . . I was big and fat, but I felt good, happy, and excited. I had always wanted a family of my own and I knew I was going to be a good mom.

My parents were not too happy that I was with my children's father, but I was so in love with him. He and I lived together off and on after I had given birth to Chadney and Kara but things did not go well. We were a young couple with two young kids, and he was stressed as he tried to take care of our family.

After one of our breakups, my kids and I lived with my parents for a while. My dad took the opportunity one day to voice his opinion about my relationship. He really did not want me to be with him. I listened to what my dad had to say but I still loved the father of my children and wanted to get back together with him. That's when my dad said I could no longer stay at their house, that I needed to leave. I took my kids and moved in with my aunt who lived down the street. We stayed with her for a few months before moving back in with him.

I had temporary jobs off and on during all of this, but it was hard to get a sitter for my kids since I did not have a regular, consistent work schedule. I was on food stamps and received twenty dollars a week in support. I became very good at being able to stretch a dollar. I would go to Sav-A-Lot and buy a pack of diapers, a pack of wipes, and a few packs of food to cook and I could make that last the week. It was crazy. Looking back, I don't know how I survived but

THE MONSTER WHO KILLED HIS FAMILY TWICE

that was how I lived for a while.

My kids' father and I eventually got married but it did not last; we divorced a little more than a year later. We stayed on good terms, and I never kept the kids from him. He saw them consistently for a few years but as they got older the visits became more sporadic, and he was not involved in their lives much once they started elementary school. There was not one main thing that ended our relationship, it was a lot of little things, which is typical in a breakup. We just grew apart.

———

Growing up, I had a lot of fun with my friends in our neighborhood and at school, but there was still a big hole in my life. For a long time, we did not have any family that lived nearby. It was just my parents, my brother Elijah, and me in Detroit.

My mom had a garden and liked to can fruit. My mom and I would also bake together, and she taught me how to cook. She took my brother and me to the park a lot and would also take us to the movies. She had a day care in our home and my love for children came from her.

I have always loved for my family to be together. I wanted to be able to visit my grandparents after school and get together for big family dinners and holiday celebrations, but they lived too far away. Holidays were especially depressing for me because I missed the fun and conversations and connection that come with spending time with family.

I have four older siblings from my dad's first marriage—three sisters and one brother. They lived in Connecticut when I was young, and we would travel to see them every once in a while. I remember watching my brother Fred play football on one trip. I adore Fred. He was so sweet and so nice to me. He would pick me up and carry me around and he always made me smile. We still have a close relationship today. I had a lot of fun during our family visits to Connecticut, but it made being apart the rest of the time that much harder.

To make up for the loneliness I felt at home, I just started adopting people. We grew close with some families at our church that we have remained friends with all these years. I was friends with the kids, so I adopted their parents as my aunts and uncles, and their grandparents as my grandparents.

My siblings in Connecticut eventually started moving to Detroit one by one and having families of their own. I felt so much happier once they were around. I would go to their houses and spend time with my new nieces and nephews. I loved getting to know my siblings and it also got me out of my house and away from my dad.

I loved the family time. I always liked Christmas, but it was even better once my sisters and Fred were there. Each year we would have a big dinner and then exchange gifts. I looked forward to everybody getting together, and not just at the holidays.

THE MONSTER WHO KILLED HIS FAMILY TWICE

Family has always been important to me, and I knew I wanted to be a mom someday. I did not know I was going to be such a young mom, but I had been taking care of kids since I was a kid myself. I helped my mom with her day care, and then I had nieces and nephews around, so I was always around babies. I already knew what to do so I was not scared at all when I got pregnant.

When I was pregnant with Kara I would talk to Chadney and tell him, "This is your little sister," and have him kiss my stomach. I took responsibility for my kids, especially when they were babies, because it was my job to take care of them. Chadney was an introvert, so I always had them together and tried to engage him at all times because I wanted us to be a close family. He was not too happy when I first brought Kara home, but I knew that was a normal response.

Kara liked to be bossy when she was little and tell her big brother what to do. I often had to tell her, "Stop bossing your brother," but Chadney could hold his own with her. If she started acting that way toward him he would tell her, "You're not the boss of me, girl."

They were so funny and I have so many stories and pictures and memories of them and the different things they would do. Every year I would take Chadney to get his picture taken and when we would get them back we would ask him, "Why do you always look so surprised?" He was just so energetic and his eyeballs were so large. He was a happy kid and full of energy.

THE MONSTER WHO KILLED HIS FAMILY TWICE

———

Parents are the primary examples in a child's life; how they act, what they say, and how they interact—with each other and with their children—shape a child's thoughts, behaviors, and how they relate to others. The effects of this continue into adulthood. That was certainly the case when I was growing up.

I was intentional about raising my kids differently from how I was raised. I said to myself—and I said this to my parents—, "I don't want to be like either one of my parents." I grew up in a very strict household. There should be rules and you need to be regimented and kids should have chores. But at the same time, you have to talk to your children. There are certain things you can't expect them to just understand. You have to communicate, and that was not something my family did well when I was growing up.

From childhood until early young adulthood, I could not really voice my opinion at home. I started speaking my mind as I got older and started having children of my own. I would stand up to my dad and say things like, "No, you're not going to treat them this way because these are my children," or "You do not get to discipline them just because you don't agree. At the end of the day, I'm still their mom." I knew how my dad had made me feel when I was young—there was a lot of shaming—and I did not want my kids to feel that way.

We never talked about our feelings when I was young. I don't remember having conversations like that. My parents might have asked, "How was your day at school?" but it did not go further than that. I took a different approach with my kids. I always allowed them to express themselves. I used to say to them, "It's okay for you to be mad. You can tell me, and I'm not going to be upset with you. We are going to talk about it and we're going to get through it. It's a part of life." I would ask them about their feelings and encouraged them to talk about how they felt.

I encouraged my kids daily. I would often tell them, "You can do anything you put your mind to." I would try to show them they had a support system by doing what I could and working with them to help them achieve their goals.

I wanted my kids to feel comfortable in their own home—not like they didn't want to be there because of me—and I would tell them so. I was not trying to be their friend, but I wanted them to feel comfortable and loved and protected at all times. I did not always have that.

I wanted them to ask questions and I would share my experiences with them, but I was careful about it. If they were not mature enough or mentally ready to hear something I would explain, "This is something I can't share with you right now." But I always believed in being open and honest with my children. If they wanted to ask anything I would say, "Sure, ask me. I'm going to tell you the truth." That's how it should be.

I wanted the best for my kids, and I was always trying to find something different for them to do and experience. I wanted to open their eyes, expose them to new things, and help them learn. Every time Chadney and Kara had something at school I tried to be there. On the days I had to work, I made sure that my sister or my parents were there so my kids had someone from their family there to support them and encourage them. I wanted them to grow up surrounded by family like I hadn't been.

Having Chadney and Kara was a blessing. I loved being a mom and I wanted to provide them with the best life possible.

4
DEVIL IN DISGUISE

The next time I saw my future husband was in 2008. I was in my thirties. He was back at Church of the Risen Christ again and he looked just as young as he had when I saw him the first time. He was still a good-looking guy, and he was nicely dressed. I was mesmerized. Those feelings I had for him when I was fourteen came rushing back.

I started talking to him after church one day and he did not know who I was at first. That was one of the facts the media got wrong: they reported that my dad had introduced me to him. The truth is, I introduced myself. When I explained that my dad was the head pastor, his response was, "Oh, wow. Okay." He had no idea I was the pastor's daughter.

A few weeks later I gave him my number. We started hanging out more and then we started dating. We weren't keeping it a secret, but no one knew we were dating. No one, including my dad—another fact the media got wrong.

It was the beginning of our relationship and we were just

getting to know each other. For about six months, we were just doing us. I was living with my parents at the time, and it was not until he started coming over to our house that they learned we were seeing each other.

As I started getting to know him I found out he had been in prison. That was not a red flag for me. Many formerly incarcerated individuals in my dad's church had gone on to do well and live successful lives and I was used to that world. My dad's assistant pastor and many of the deacons had been incarcerated. What I saw all around me was that men who make mistakes can change.

When I asked him about his time in prison, he said there had been an incident with his wife; they had gotten into an argument, and she attacked him. He tried to defend himself without hurting her but in doing so she fell and hit her head and was killed. He said it was an accident and I took him at his word.

I saw that he was going to church and trying to get himself together. In my dad's church, being formerly incarcerated was not considered a badge of shame. My dad did not hide that he himself had been in prison, and he didn't hide it about anyone else in his church either.

My dad would let it be known if someone had been incarcerated, but he would not go beyond that. He would not reveal anything specific about someone's past, only that they had been in prison and they were welcome at his church. That's how it was with him. People knew he was

THE MONSTER WHO KILLED HIS FAMILY TWICE

previously incarcerated, but they did not know the details—the opposite of what the media reported.

My boyfriend moved in with me and things were fine at first. He did not like talking about his family or his childhood much, but I just figured it must have been bad, that maybe it was dysfunctional and uncomfortable for him and hard to talk about. He was always nice and seemed like he would be a good husband. That was why I could not explain it at the time—I have a hard time explaining it now—but I kept feeling like something wasn't right. We had only been living together for a few months when I decided to break it off with him.

I did not talk to him for close to a year. Then in December 2009 he called to ask me what Chadney and Kara wanted for Christmas. That was the beginning of us slowly getting back together. He bought them what they asked for, a skateboard for Chadney and a PSP handheld game for Kara. My ex called me again for New Year's and then the next day he took me out for breakfast. Kara sang in the choir at school, and in February he came to hear her perform at the Fox Theater. Not long after that I learned I was pregnant with my third child.

I took a pregnancy test and two lines appeared in the test window in an instant. I put my hand on my forehead and looked away from the test stick. I kept trying to convince myself that it would change from two lines—pregnant—to one line—not pregnant. I looked at the test stick several more times and each time it still showed two lines. I was in disbelief. I thought, *This can't be happening right now. The timing is crazy. Now I have to tell this man that I am pregnant.*

He was happy about the news. He came to my doctor appointments with me and when we found out we were having a girl, anything I needed for her he bought for her. I don't know if I ignored it or it just went away, but I no longer had that strange uneasy feeling about him from before. It just wasn't there anymore.

Our daughter Koi was born on October 28, 2010 and her father was all in. He was mesmerized and so in love with her from day one. I was living with my parents, and he would come over every day to see her and hold her. I could tell he was really happy.

After I had Koi, her father started talking about wanting to get married. I spoke to my dad about it and he said we should get married, but that we needed to go to pre-marital counseling first. That was the requirement at his church; an engaged couple was supposed to go to counseling for a year before they got married.

My mom was a pastor at the church and he and I did our counseling with her for about six months. Then he got a job with the city of Detroit and we weren't able to meet with her after that. He just worked, that's the type of person he was. It was one of the main topics we had discussed in pre-marital counseling. We were going to be a blended family with Koi and Chadney and Kara, and he needed to understand that he could not just work to pay the bills and let everything else fall on me. It would take effort from both of us.

My dad performed our wedding ceremony on December 18, 2010.

5

TORMENT

My husband and I lived with my parents for almost a year after we got married so we could save money to buy our own house. Starting our new life together was a big adjustment for him. We were learning to live as a married couple; we were learning to live as a blended family; and my husband was a father for the first time.

He would often give me a hard time about how I took care of Koi. If I held her, he would tell me to put her down. If she cried, he would tell me to nurse her—he was constantly telling me to nurse her, whether she was crying or not. I finally said to him, "This is not my first child. I know what to do with babies. I had two before and I have been taking care of kids since I was nine."

My husband did not want me to go anywhere or do anything without Koi. If I needed to run an errand or wanted to visit one of my siblings or adopted aunts or grandparents he would say, "You have to take Koi with you." He insisted on it. On top of that he continued pushing me to nurse her and did not want me to switch to bottle feeding her. It all became too much for me and the stress started to show. The bags under my eyes became so dark that a family member asked if my husband was beating me. He wasn't. I was just physically and mentally exhausted.

Things were not going well for our new family, and I felt overwhelmed. I knew I had to do something to give myself some relief, so I decided to go back to work. I found a job at Target doing early morning stocking from 4:00 a.m. to 10:00 a.m.

I had been thinking about leaving my husband around the time I started my new job when I found out I was pregnant again. Our second daughter, Kaleigh, was born September 5, 2012.

My husband was much different with Kaleigh than he had been when Koi was born. He would hold Kaleigh every once in a while, but he never wanted to feed her. It took him longer to engage with her and I could see that he was acting distant with her. When I asked him why he said it was because he had wanted a boy. I told him, "Well, you have a girl and she's here now. So what are you going to do? You can't act like that."

He had made nursing such a bad experience with Koi that I knew I could not go through that a second time. I decided I would not nurse Kaleigh; I was still in the hospital after giving birth to her when I learned that we could get formula through the supplemental nutrition program for Women, Infants, and Children (WIC). My husband had been so adamant about me nursing Koi that I knew he would not like my decision, so I put off telling him. When I finally discussed it with him, the conversation did not go well.

I was talking to him on the phone while I was still in the hospital and explained what I had decided. He tried to talk me out of it. He said he would be different this time, but I was not going to take any chances. I told him I could not go through that again and I stood by my decision. Then I asked him to buy some formula because I would not be discharged in time to get it before the store closed.

I thought it was a simple request, so I was shocked when my husband started yelling at me. I had to get out of bed and lock myself in my hospital bathroom, stretching the phone cord across the room as I did, because Kara was in the room with me and she could hear him yelling. I was so embarrassed my daughter had to witness that.

I did not understand why my husband was so angry and why he couldn't just buy a can of formula. After we got off the phone, I called my mother in tears because I was so confused by his behavior. That was just the beginning.

My husband and I had finally saved up enough money by living with my parents that we could afford to buy a place of our own. We signed the papers in the hospital right after I had given birth to Kaleigh and then moved in and started to settle in as a family of six. Chadney was in high school and

Kara was in middle school; I stayed home to take care of Koi and Kaleigh while my husband worked.

When Koi was a baby we went as a family to my dad's church, but after a while my husband stopped going with us. I started taking my kids to a different church; my parents were not happy about that, but I did what was best for my family. Every week Koi would beg my husband to join us. She would say, "Daddy, go to church with us," but he would always tell her, "I have to go to work." The service wasn't that long, and he would have made it to work on time, but he never would go.

Things at our new house were okay in the beginning. We would watch TV together and sometimes we would have a family night or take the kids to the movies. At times my husband could be really nice, but it was not long before he was criticizing the way I talked to the kids or how I took care of them. If I would tell them to do something he would say they didn't have to listen to me, and he always tried to correct the way I did things.

After a few months, his attitude really started to change. There were times he would get really quiet—so quiet that it was weird. He simply refused to speak. Then the opposite would happen. Everything would be fine one minute and all of a sudden something would set him off and he would get so angry. There were many times I had no idea what he was angry about.

THE MONSTER WHO KILLED HIS FAMILY TWICE

It takes time for new parents to adjust, no matter how many children you have. It was still early in our marriage, and we had two young babies and two teenagers. It was a lot, so I chalked my husband's behavior up to the changes we were navigating and the stress that came from that. No marriage is perfect, and it takes work to have a successful relationship. I wanted a family, and I was willing to do the work, which meant trying to understand my husband and find a way to help him if I could.

I wanted to help him, but I did not know how. His unexplained outbursts of anger followed by long bouts of silence, and his frequent criticisms of how I parented our kids continued. I would ask him what had happened, why he was upset, but he would just stare at me in complete silence with a cold, hard look in his eyes. Things did not improve. When I was growing up, I would do anything to get out of the house, away from my dad. Now I was feeling the same way about my husband.

One day I needed water for Kaleigh's formula so I asked my husband to buy some, but he wouldn't do it. Several days later he finally walked in with a gallon of water. I could not understand what was going through his head. If I had left it up to him our baby would have been starving. What kind of person would do that to their child?

I went back to work, which forced my husband to be more hands-on with Kaleigh. He finally started to engage with her, and she slowly began to grow on him, but it was still nothing like the closeness he felt for Koi.

My husband was better with Chadney and Kara at first. When we were dating, he would pick them up from school. He would go to Chadney's football games and Kara's choir performances and their other activities. He was involved. But things changed once we moved into our own house.

It started with something so minor: my husband did not like how Kara closed her bedroom door. I could not figure out what the problem was. Something about the sound of the latch clicking into place seemed to trigger him. He would get so angry and accuse Kara of slamming her door when all she had done was close it. It was yet another small thing that set him off, and as usual his reaction was over the top.

I had started a new contract job and things at home grew progressively worse. My husband would argue with me and yell at me and I had no idea why. His moods would change in an instant. We could be sitting on the couch watching TV and everything would be fine. Then I would leave the room for a minute or two and when I would come back his attitude had changed for the worse. I was so confused. I would ask, "What happened between me walking to the other room and coming back?" He would just stare at me with a crazy look on his face.

I didn't know what to do when he was like that so I would just leave him alone. I thought, *Maybe he's having a bad day*. I figured something was going on and he did not know how to express it so he was taking it out on me. Just when I thought

THE MONSTER WHO KILLED HIS FAMILY TWICE

it could not get any worse, it finally did.

Early in the day one day, my husband was mad about something - even now I don't know what set him off. At one point he accused me of trying to take the tax money. It was being deposited into his account so that would not have even been possible. But he was on a rampage, and it escalated throughout the day.

My husband and I had stopped sleeping in the same bed together a long time ago and on this particular night I was sleeping on the couch with Kaleigh when he came into the living room yelling at me and woke me up. He called me a bitch and kept going on and on. He was a big man, and he was out of control. I did not know what to do so I sat there and endured it.

He was enraged, and I kept telling him he needed to stop yelling because the kids were asleep. That was when he started kicking the couch. All I could think about was Kaleigh's safety. He continued to kick the couch and act crazy; at one point he was holding Koi and I tried to get him to put her down. He finally laid her on a pallet we had on the living room floor and went back into his room.

I was stunned. I knew I could not take the mental torment anymore and that I needed to get my kids out of this toxic environment. My husband had gone too far. I did not get any sleep the rest of the night as I lay there and tried to figure out what to do.

I left a little early for work the next day—but not too

early. I did not want my husband to get suspicious. I went to the police station to file a police report but when I got there it was closed. I tried again a few days later. This time an officer told me I could not file a complaint there, I had to go to the municipal building downtown and file a personal protection order (PPO). That was not too far from where I worked so I took an extended lunch that day and walked there. I filled out the paperwork—there was a lot of it—and handed it to the clerk. She came back a few minutes later and said I had not provided enough information, that these incidents had to happen multiple times before the police could respond. She said there was nothing they could do. At this point I did not know the truth about my husband's past, so the insanity of what she was telling me did not occur to me until much later.

My plan for a PPO had failed but I still knew I did not want my kids in that household any longer. They were witnesses as my husband raged and argued with me for no reason and cussed me out; the saw his odd silences when he refused to speak. I noticed that Koi was so nervous she had started to bite her nails. The kids were often confused by mixed messages from their parents as my husband would always undermine me. Those are just a few examples of the ongoing torment he put us through. There were more.

There was the time I was in my room and Kaleigh came in carrying a loaf of bread. She liked to eat bread and butter—she called it peanut butter—and wanted me to

THE MONSTER WHO KILLED HIS FAMILY TWICE

make her some. I was in the middle of doing something so I said, "Give me a minute and I'll make you some. Go put the bread back on the kitchen counter." A few minutes later we were all in the kitchen and my husband asked who had smushed the bread. I said, "Oh, probably Kaleigh because I told her to put it back on the counter. She's so little it's hard for her to reach so she probably smushed it."

The next thing I knew my husband was lunging across the kitchen trying to get to Kaleigh. I moved as quick as I could to get between them, but he was still able to reach her and he slapped her so hard on her side. I was furious. I yelled, "If you ever put your fucking hands on her again I will fuck you up. You're going to hit her over some bread? She's a baby. So what if she smushed some bread? It's not ruined. Would you treat Koi this way?"

My husband was still so captivated by Koi, and he still did not feel the same about Kaleigh. For some reason he had it out for her. When I would call him on it and ask, "She's a baby, what could she have done to you?" he would just say, "She doesn't listen." I would try to explain to him that kids are not going to listen and that he could not show favoritism, but it was something he never understood. My husband also had an issue with Kara. He picked on her a lot, for no reason—and he did not like it at all that Koi idolized Kara.

One day I came home from work and as soon as I opened the door I smelled gas—the odor was strong. I went into the kitchen and saw the knobs on the stove were on, so I turned them off right away. I looked for my husband to ask him about it and found him sitting on the couch with Koi and Kaleigh. I said, "You don't smell the gas?" He tried to blame it on Kara or Chadney but I knew they had not used the stove before going to school; then he tried to blame Koi. It was only later that he finally admitted he had been thinking about killing himself. I was upset but I tried to stay calm. I wanted him to tell me what was going on . . . what was going through his head. I asked, "Why would you do that when the girls were in the house?" but he never gave me a real answer. I did not know what to do and I didn't want to upset him any further. All I could think was, *What if I had not come home in time?*

My husband continued to wake me up at night to yell at me. Sometimes I would not even know what he was talking about at first. If I had a confused look on my face he would say, "Don't frown your face at me." I would tell him, "You can't just wake me up in the middle of the night and expect me to be coherent and be able to have a conversation." There was one night when he would just not leave me alone, so I finally had to sleep outside on the swing Chadney had given me for my birthday one year.

I felt helpless. I had wanted a husband and a family for so long and I was trying my best with my husband. My first and main example of what a relationship between a husband and wife was like was of course my mom and dad. I saw them have some good times together but a lot of the time I saw my dad being mean and pushy with my mom. She was quiet when she was around him. Very often he would not let her talk when they were having discussions or disagreements. He would talk over her and tell her she wasn't right. It made me nervous when he would raise his voice with her. He would not yell at her; he just had a look in his eyes, or he would point his finger in her face. I didn't like that. I always believed if two people are having a conversation, no matter what it is about, both people should be able to express how they feel.

I had watched my parents argue, but they stayed together. I was trying to do the same. I wanted to understand my husband and communicate with him. But the night that ended with him kicking the couch where Kaleigh was sleeping was more than I could take. My efforts at trying to make our marriage and our family work were of no use. It was time to take my kids and leave.

I continued to work and started saving my money. I informed my parents that I planned to leave with the kids on the last day of school so I would not disrupt their education. I made reservations with a moving company and had a crew and a truck ready to go on June 13, 2013.

When my husband left for work that day, I waited an hour to make sure he was not going to come back. Then the movers and my parents arrived. We packed up the house within two hours and I left to pick the kids up from school.

6
ONE MORE YEAR

My kids and I moved in with my parents for a little while before I got us our own place. My husband was mad at first and he cut off our cell phones—mine, Chadney's, and Kara's—but I still kept in contact with him because of Koi and Kaleigh. We had to talk about their schedules and their school and all the things that come with having children together.

I had started divorce proceedings, and while that was going on we agreed that my husband's older sister would pick the girls up at my parents' house and take them to see my husband. That lasted for a month or two and then my husband and I started meeting on our own to exchange the girls. He would take them every other weekend and sometimes when he was off work.

Then we slowly started to talk again, about more than just the kids. And instead of staring back at me in an eerie silence, my husband was really making an effort to communicate. We started to discuss our problems in detail. Having a blended family was still hard for him and we talked through a lot of those issues.

Then one day, after a meeting we had both attended at Koi's school, we kept looking at each other and something felt different. In time we decided that we were going to try to work things out. We moved back in with my husband in September 2015. We lived together as a family for one more year.

Everything seemed okay the next few months and my husband was in a good mood. He likes Christmas, and he was really into it that year. He bought Koi and Kaleigh Hello Kitty cars, bikes, and all kinds of toys. We had a nice New Year's, too, but I could tell my husband was having a hard time after that. Then things got progressively worse.

My husband started making comments about me having a boyfriend. I am not the type of person that would cheat but even if I was, I did not have time to cheat. I was a stay-at-home mom at this point. I was with my husband during the day until he went to work and then I was at home with Koi and Kaleigh. I was busy taking them to ballet and cheer. Kara was in the National Honor Society and always involved in all types of activities. I took the kids to church on the weekends, and I had girlfriends of my own that I would hang out with. Our life was full of school, homework, and activities.

My husband began picking on Kara again and continued to get upset about the way she shut her bedroom door. I wondered if it had something to do with the way his cell had locked when he was in prison because I could just not figure out why that bothered him so much. It got so bad that one day Chadney called me at work. "He took the doorknob off her door," he said. It was not the first time my husband had done this. I called him and asked what was going on. He said, "See, you're taking her side," and then hung up on me. I tried to ask him about it again when I got home later but it just escalated into an argument.

One day my husband came upstairs from the basement upset that someone had put his clothes in the dryer and demanded to know who had done it. I said, "Kara put your clothes in the dryer. I hung your work pants up and then turned the dryer on." He started yelling at Kara and said, "I'm going to fuck you up." I rushed to get between them and protect my child.

It didn't make any sense. All Kara did was put his clothes in the dryer. I was about to push him but he is a big guy and I did not want him to push me back. He continued mouthing off to Kara and she was talking back to him. I told her not to say another word and then I focused my attention on my husband. "You are not going to put your hands on my child. I don't even know what is happening right now. I don't know why you are upset. You are just going to go to the back room and calm down."

Kara went down to the basement and discovered that my husband had taken her laundry out of the washing machine and thrown it all over the floor. I went to ask my husband about it because it was so messed up. He refused to say a word. That same day he called Kara a bitch. He still would not answer me when I asked him what the problem was. He just had it out for Kara. None of it made any sense.

My husband had also started picking on Kaleigh again. If he was watching TV with Koi, he did not want Kaleigh in there with them. One time he shut the door in her face to keep her out, which really hurt her feelings. Kaleigh cried a lot and that really annoyed him. Instead of trying to help her he would just tell her to go to her room. If he ever asked her to do something and she told him no, he would make a quick, threatening gesture at her, but Kaleigh was feisty and tough and would always stand up to him. I would step in immediately and put a stop to it whenever I saw him do it.

Koi had started kindergarten when we moved back in with my husband and for the entire school year he told her she did not have to go to school if she didn't want to. Many days he would call me at work to say Koi was not going to school that day. We fought about it the entire year. She was struggling from so many absences that I called to let the teacher know what he was telling Koi and that he was fighting me on the issue.

I was driving her to school one day when she told me she didn't need to go. I thought, *This is crazy. My five-year-old kid is telling me she doesn't need school and her dad tells her it's okay. Unless she is sick, she doesn't need to be at home, she needs to be in school.*

We finally enrolled her at the Sylvan Learning Center and got her a tutor and she went to summer school after that. It took a lot to get her up to speed.

Things at home had gotten so bad that once again I did not want to be there. I was working, which got me out of the house for a little while each day, but I had had it by now. I started taking some classes so I would be home even less.

I knew I could not be in a marriage like this and that it was not fair to my kids either. I never talked bad about my husband to my kids, but I would always be honest with them when they asked me questions. Kara overheard my husband call me a bitch one time and asked me about it later. I do not believe in lying so I said, "Yeah, he did say that. I'm sorry you had to hear it." When my husband would get upset for no reason I would explain to them, "What he is doing is not how a dad is supposed to treat his children or treat Mom."

I had told my parents and a few friends about what had been happening when things started getting bad and they understood that I wanted to make my marriage work. My mother and a friend both told me to stand my ground and not leave my house. My father said, "Well, you can't come here again." I thought, *That's fine because this time I'm moving directly into my own place.* I did not care about staying in the house.

I told my kids we were going to be moving out for good because I did not want them to be in that environment anymore. I started looking for a full-time job and began the process of filing for divorce again.

A month later, Chadney and I were sitting on the couch wondering what my husband was about to do next.

7

THE TRAGEDY

My husband pulled a big bag of zip ties out of his back pocket and said, "Chad, I want you to tie up your mom." I don't know if I went into shock right then and there, but I could not say a word. Chadney tried to reason with my husband but he pulled out a gun and pointed it at my son. I did not know where the gun had come from - we didn't even own one. All I could think was I did not want my son to get hurt. In that moment my protective instinct overrode my shock and I found my voice. I said, "Chadney, just do what he says."

Chadney did not zip-tie my wrists too tight but after my husband tied Chadney's wrists, he tied mine even tighter. My son kept talking to him the entire time trying to change his mind about what he was doing to us.

I had put Koi and Kaleigh to bed a few hours before and Kara was in the bathroom getting ready for bed while this was going on. She had finished taking a shower and my husband told her she needed to hurry up and come to the living room. I kept a calm voice and said, "Can I talk to you?" He said, "Yeah, what's up?" I asked if he would let Kara put some clothes on. He said, "Yeah, I can let her do that for you."

Kara came into the living room a few minutes later with a look on her face like, "What the heck?" Her phone kept dinging and all I could see in my mind was my husband getting annoyed with her and hitting her with the gun. I didn't say a word, I just made eye contact with her and kept shaking my head thinking, *No. Do not answer that phone . . . do not touch that phone.* My husband had her sit on the couch next to Chadney and me and he zip-tied her, too, and he just kept talking and talking the entire time. At one point he said he was going to take us to the basement, and he asked us if we knew what hog tie meant because that's what he was going to do to us.

He took us downstairs and had us lay on the basement floor, then he duct-taped our mouths, wrists, ankles, and around our knees putting extra duct tape on me. He continued to talk the entire time, but I was not paying attention. My mind was focused on figuring out a way to get out of this and how I could keep my kids safe.

At one point I heard him say, "Your mom was cheating on me." He had accused me of this often after we had moved back in; it was never true, but I could not convince him of that. I also heard him say, "I don't want the girls" - meaning Koi and Kaleigh - "being raised by anyone in your family. I don't want them to be like Kara." He got a little angry as he mentioned Kara, but his voice became normal again as he kept on talking. A little while later he slid down from where he was sitting on the counter and walked back upstairs.

Chadney and I were able to loosen the tape on our mouths so we could talk. The first thing he said to me was, "Mom, did you cheat? Did you cheat?" I said, "No, I did not. You know I am not going to lie. Even if it's embarrassing, I am not going to lie to you."

There was nothing I could do to help any of us at that point, but I was trying to come up with a plan. I thought if we heard my husband close the front door to the house we could try to free each other and then use the phone in the basement to call the police. I kept waiting and listening for the sound of the front door closing but he just kept going in and out of the basement, talking the entire time.

Sometimes my mom would get weird feelings about someone, so I prayed for that to happen. I prayed for anyone to help us. When he asked me, "Do you want to see the girls?" I felt a tear roll down my face as I nodded my head yes. He put a white mattress pad down on the floor and then said, "No, that's going to be too much." I thought, *Here we go again. You're being lazy,* but I had no idea what he had done with Koi and Kaleigh. At this point I just thought he was going to take them and leave.

Time just seemed to stand still. He never brought Koi and Kaleigh down to the basement. He just kept talking, going upstairs, and coming back downstairs. The entire time he never said what he was going to do, just that he was going to call the police when he got done.

He eventually removed the duct tape from our mouths and then picked me up like I was a doll and sat me down on the couch. The rest of me was still duct-taped so all I could do was watch as he turned and pointed the gun at my daughter. I screamed, "My baby . . . no! Don't shoot her!" I saw the soundwaves from the gun as he fired two shots into Kara's back. There was nothing I could do to save her. She died instantly. I will never get the sound of that gun going off out of my head.

I could tell that my husband struggled when he went over to my son. He did not want to shoot Chadney. He would point the gun at him and then lower it; he did this several times before he finally pulled the trigger. Chadney said, "Ouch," and rolled over. Then my husband walked over and stood in front of me.

I was trying to brace myself but there was nothing I could do. He shot at me twice. I felt a burning sensation as a bullet ricocheted and grazed two of my toes on my right foot. Then he grabbed my face and cut me. I could not feel the blade slice my cheek, but I felt and saw the blood. He made a move to cut me again and I shook my head no. Then he threw the box cutter down, put the gun on a barstool, and walked over to the phone in the basement.

I could hear the other end of the call. The first one rang

and rang and finally went to voicemail. He made a second call and his niece answered. He told her in a normal, calm voice, "The girls are no longer here. They're in heaven." When she asked "What?" he repeated himself. I heard her say, "Oh, my God. What did you do? Where is Faith? Let me speak to her." He said, "Oh, I left her alive," and then put the phone to my ear. She asked me what was going on and all I could say was, "He killed the kids," and then I started crying.

The next thing I knew my husband had gone upstairs where I heard him call 911 and speak to the operator, still in that normal, calm voice. Then he hung up the phone and waited for the police to arrive. I did not know if he was going to come back to the basement, so I pretended like I was dead. It seemed like forever again, but he never returned.

I have not spoken to him since.

8

ANSWERS AND QUESTIONS

"Is anybody down here?" The police were standing at the top of the basement stairs announcing themselves. I called out to let them know I was there, and they told me to come upstairs. "I'm tied up . . . I can't," I called out again, so they came down to me.

My hands were numb, and the police could not tell where I was bleeding from at first. At some point emergency responders put a neck brace on me and then I was being taken to the hospital. That was where I found out that my husband had taken Koi and Kaleigh out of their beds, put them in his car, and killed them by carbon monoxide poisoning. Now I understood why he had parked so close to the house, and why he had cleaned up the garage and the carport the day before.

More things started to make sense as I lay in my hospital room. The hospital staff asked me if I wanted to see my two youngest daughters. I said yes and a nurse helped me into a wheelchair and took me into Koi's room first. I sat by her bed and held her hand. She was very, very cold. When the nurse wheeled me into Kaleigh's room, her little hand was still warm as I held it, and it made me think of something my husband had said earlier that night: "Kaleigh is a fighter." I did not know what he meant at the time, but when I was being taken out of the house on a gurney, I had seen the paramedics working on her. She had been fighting very hard for her life but the EMTs were not able to save my baby.

During one of the many times my husband was walking in and out of the basement that night, he had come downstairs to where we were tied up and I heard him crying. It sounded weird and fake to me, and I thought he was pretending. I realized in the hospital that was probably when Koi and Kaleigh were gone and he got the nerve to come back into the house and do what he did to us.

―――――

It is reasonable for someone who hears bits and pieces of my story to say, "My God, he killed his first wife and you had kids with him and married him and your father knew it and married you two anyway?" That is a fair criticism. But it is also why people are not supposed to rush to judgment until we have all the facts.

People have made comments on forums and social media such as, "Why would she marry him right out of prison?" That was not how it happened. People have said,

"She deserves what she got." Those comments are hurtful, because those people do not know the whole story.

The media reported that the first time my husband was in prison I had gone there and advocated for his early release. The truth is, I was fourteen years old at the time that occurred. I had only seen him a few times at church; I never spoke to him back then and I did not know why he was not there anymore.

I also never knew the truth about what my husband had done to his first wife and neither did my family. It was not until journalists started releasing information in the hours and days following the tragedy in 2015 that I, and my family, learned the truth about my husband's past.

To this day I still don't know the whole story. I was reading an article about it online and learned that his first wife was about six months pregnant when he stabbed her multiple times. I knew my husband had been married before and that they were having problems, but he never disclosed to me that she was pregnant, and he never said that he stabbed her. All that was running through my head when I read the article was, *Oh my God . . . oh my God*. I could not read any more of it and I have not read a word about it since. What he did to her was horrible.

People have wondered why my family let me marry a man who had killed his first wife and unborn child. They didn't. Yes, we knew my husband had been incarcerated. But he manipulated and deceived us all. If my family had thought my husband was a threat to the extent that he was, they would have stepped in long before the tragedy. Our family has been around formerly incarcerated individuals for years, many of whom are leading productive lives today. None of us saw this coming.

My dad knew more details than any of us did, but he is also a man of faith. As a man of faith, his stance was, "We're going to give my husband a second chance." People want to know why my dad would write letters in support of my husband's early release from prison if he did not know all the details of what my husband had done. The answer is, I don't know.

What is the faith-based community's role in welcoming formerly incarcerated individuals? It depends on who you ask. There is no standard. Each pastor and each faith group determine what their approach is going to be.

If a formerly incarcerated person wants to attend services at a church, there is sometimes a connection between the church and the organization overseeing their release, such as a probation officer. Some church leaders believe they have a responsibility to their congregation, that if you were formerly incarcerated and you're in a church fellowship you should not have a problem with your church family knowing about your past, especially if you have changed.

Other church leaders feel their responsibility is to introduce formerly incarcerated individuals to Christ and a better way of life. They usually accept the person's

THE MONSTER WHO KILLED HIS FAMILY TWICE

story about their past. They try to be careful not to say, "Joe here is a child molester, watch out for him." Rather, "This is Joe. Welcome him, embrace him, and greet him into the fellowship." Giving individuals a second chance is fundamental in Christianity, and that was the approach I believe my dad chose. Unfortunately, my husband betrayed my dad, the church, and sadly, me and my children.

I did not know anything about the letters my dad wrote until September 21, 2016, as I lay in my hospital bed and heard it mentioned on the news. The media reported otherwise—that I had known about the letters all along—but that is another detail they got wrong.

I asked my dad about the letters not too long ago. While he did say that my husband had come to him and told him that he had accidentally killed his wife, I did not get any real answers. That could be because my dad is eighty-two and at times he has problems with his memory. But I also wonder if he is just not able to face the reality of what happened. The truth is I really don't know. I don't know how long my father kept in touch with my husband after he went to prison the first time. I don't know the extent of their relationship. I don't know how much he knew about my husband's past. I have the same questions that many people do. I don't have the answers.

What I do know is that my husband lied to me, to my family, and to the members of my dad's church. We took him at his word, and we were blindsided.

I did not want to move back in with my husband as soon as I did in 2015. We were going to take our time and try dating again and go from there. I really wanted to date until Kara graduated from high school in May 2017. But for some reason my water bill at my apartment kept getting higher and higher. I had the maintenance guy come out to take a look; he could not find any leaks, but my bill just kept increasing to the point where I could no longer afford to pay it. That was the first time in my life I had ever had any utility cut off. We did not have water that entire summer so we would either go to my parents' house to shower or I would buy gallons of water and heat them up. The people who owned the place lived out of the country and were not willing to work with me on a payment plan.

It was September when my husband said, "You might as well come back home and move your things back here because it's starting to get cold." I thought, *He has a point. What am I going to do when October, November, December come? The pipes will freeze.*

That was part of the reason I moved back in with my husband. The other part was because despite the mental and verbal torture, there was a side of him that was charming and nice. That was why I started dating him in the first place. I also went back because I wanted to make my marriage work.

I wanted to be married and have a family. My husband could be very sweet, and we did have some good times. I liked when he would interact with us and laugh and joke around. Sometimes he would tell me about something that happened when he was little or a memory he had from when he was in school when he was young. Those were the good times.

I did love my husband, I would not have married him if I didn't. And love does not just go away. I felt we could really make our marriage work—at least he made be believe we could. I did not expect things to be perfect, but he was supposed to love me back. He was supposed to guide me and protect me and be a good father to our children and a good husband. But he was not any of those things.

I tried to find out more about his past after we were married, and I did take steps to protect my children. I spoke with an attorney who sent me to a website where I could not access any information, and after that he brushed me off.

When the judge denied my PPO I thought, *So I basically have to wait until he beats my ass or does something worse.* Now I think, *Those people knew my husband was a convicted murderer and they told me I didn't have enough information to get a PPO? Really?*

I spoke with a family advocate during my two-year separation from my husband and told her some of my concerns. Her response was, "Well, what's wrong with that?" My efforts to get help proved to be futile. It is a hard place to be in when you are trying to get help and people make you feel like you are the one doing something wrong.

Would I have tried harder to find out about his past if

THE MONSTER WHO KILLED HIS FAMILY TWICE

I could do it over again? Of course. Would I have moved my kids back in with him if I could have foreseen that he really had not changed in two years? Never. Those are easy questions to answer today. That can be said of anyone looking back on their life.

There are more important things that need to be talked about from a domestic violence perspective rather than why people stay in those situations or why they go back. The real questions should focus on the abusers and the criminal justice system—not the victims. My husband killed his first wife and unborn child and was released from prison. Is that justice?

The majority of domestic violence cases don't go anywhere. If there is talk of physical violence—threats of violence—it is rare you will see justice. Why does it have to get to murder first? Because forensic evidence points to homicide; with aggravated assault there are often no witnesses, and the case is reliant on the victim's testimony.

As I watched the interrogation tapes after the tragedy, I saw footage of my husband going into Home Depot and buying the supplies he would use to kill Koi and Kaleigh. It was almost as though God was trying to intervene and give him a chance to change his mind. For some reason my husband's card wouldn't go through when he was trying to pay. He tried three times unsuccessfully. The fourth time it finally worked.

THE MONSTER WHO KILLED HIS FAMILY TWICE

The man I saw in the interrogation video was a man I did not know. When he shot Kara twice in the back, they were death shots—she never had a chance. The police asked him how he knew to shoot like that and he replied, "I guess just from watching TV." He said it matter-of-factly, showing no remorse. They asked him if he had gotten treatment when he was in the prison the first time. He said, "Yeah, but you just tell them what they want to hear." My jaw dropped when I heard that. I was in disbelief. He was an entirely different person than I had ever seen before.

When he said on the video that what he did to me was destined, all I could think was, *Who says that? Who does that? I didn't do anything*. That was when I realized, all of those times we had met to exchange the girls while we were separated, he already had an agenda.

After the tragedy, one of my husband's close friends apologized to me. He told me, "He did say he was going to do this, but I thought he was just talking." That was sometime between 2013 and 2015. I guess he tried to give him the benefit of the doubt, thinking he was just blowing off steam.

―――――

When I walked into the courtroom during his trial, the officers there that day offered to go in front of me to protect me. my husband was within arm's reach of me and he probably could have tried something, but I thought, *I'm not scared of him*. I was ready.

9
STARTING OVER

Right after the tragedy I was just existing. I was on medication and drinking and partying. My memory was affected by the trauma I had just been through, but the medication made it even worse. I started sleeping with a piece of wood or a mallet under my pillow because—especially at nighttime—noises would freak me out. I was paranoid a lot of the time. If it got too bad or I became too depressed I would wind up in a closet or the bathroom with my pillow and blanket. That was how I survived.

In time I started dating someone and it was fine in the beginning. I enjoyed our conversations, and he had a gentle way about him. But then he started doing things I did not agree with. A few times he suggested that we try cocaine. I thought, *I'm messed up, but I'm not messed up to the point that I'm going to try drugs.* Then he started to get possessive. I was reeling from the tragedy and making poor decisions but deep down I still had enough sense to know I was not going down that road.

I ended the relationship and became even more lonely after that. The pain I felt without my children ran so deep and hurt so much that I just wanted to die. My kids were my world. I was hurting and trying my best to cope.

It wasn't long before I reconnected with a childhood friend and started dating him; we got married a few months later. I can see now that I was trying to fill a void, but back then I was lost. I did not know if I was coming or going. I did not know what to do without my children. I wasn't aware of it at the time, but I had started taking my anger at my ex out on my new husband. My second marriage only lasted for about a year.

My family did not agree with me getting married again, and I know now that it was too soon. They were afraid for me, and I understand their fear, but what are the chances that something like that would happen again to the same person? Even though it's a scary world, I wanted my family to imagine how I felt. I had it a thousand times harder than the rest of them. I am the one who had to start all over again and heal. I felt like I had been dropped off in some foreign land and I had to learn the language and learn how to survive all on my own.

In the midst of all of the drinking and the medication and being severely depressed to the point where I couldn't eat or sleep and losing a lot of weight and acting crazy, I finally realized I had to stop. I had to find a way to push through because I did not want to be that person anymore. I kept

THE MONSTER WHO KILLED HIS FAMILY TWICE

thinking to myself, *I don't want to stay stuck like this*. I did not like how the medication made me feel so I quit taking it, and I stopped drinking.

I was seeing a psychiatrist every week and a domestic violence counselor at first. Today I have a really good therapist who I like a lot. She has taught me how to meditate. I would rather do that to deal with my stress and anxiety than take some medicine that makes me feel strange.

My therapist has also taught me how trauma affects your brain, how it starts shrinking the brain, which is why I have memory problems. It is hard for me to focus today. Sometimes I lose my train of thought and sometimes I have to ask people to repeat something they just told me, but it has improved a lot.

I started feeling better when I went back to working again because it helps take my mind off what happened. I can't ever really avoid it and I still have to deal with it but staying busy at work helps to some degree.

You're not the same anymore after experiencing a tragedy like mine. Everything changes. I am still social but sometimes I get overwhelmed, or my anxiety kicks in. That's when I say, "I'm not going to go," or "I'm not going to do that," and I am okay with that. I do not want to be somewhere where I don't know how I'm going to react. I would rather be at home where I feel at peace and relaxed.

I have not been to church in a long time. I believe there is a God or a Higher Power, but there are just some things

I do not understand. It is hard for me to say what the faith community's role in welcoming formerly incarcerated individuals should be. It is a very fine line. How can you know if someone has truly changed? When people are in prison and convert to Islam or Christianity, some stick with it when they are released, and some revert right back to their old ways. I do not know if I would welcome a relationship right away with someone who has been in prison. They have to prove themselves. I don't know how they are to do that but no matter what, we have to check into people more. We have to be more careful.

Women—and we can't leave out men, because men go through it, too—we have to open our eyes, especially when there are children involved. We have to learn the signs and they need to be taught in the home and in school.

When I was in high school I never knew that type of behavior existed until I saw a guy who I thought was really nice twist a girl's arm and slam her into a locker. I could not believe he was doing that, but some other students told me he did it all the time. It blew my mind.

Violence like that happens more frequently than we like to think. We can't wait until our kids are older; we need to start teaching them about relationships and domestic violence when they are young. That includes talking about good touches and bad touches and sex and other forms of violence and abuse—we need to start these conversations early.

THE MONSTER WHO KILLED HIS FAMILY TWICE

It is sad that we have to overload our kids with that kind of information, but we must. Not only are there male and female predators out in society but abuse also exists in the home. It could be from a parent or a sibling or another relative or family friend. We have to be talking about that. There should be some sort of school for it, so kids know the signs and know what to look out for. We can't just chalk it up to someone having a bad day or being moody. We really need to know, because our lives are at stake.

People often rely on background checks. Okay, do a background check. Maybe something comes back. But what if something doesn't? You don't know what someone is going through mentally. There are a lot of people that go undetected so you can't just say, "Oh, nothing came up on the radar, so he's good." He, or she, could be the one that is going to snap.

We need to know ourselves and we need to inform each other, even if it is just close friends or family members. When we see something, we have to speak up.

I loved my ex the best way I knew love to be. I should have found out more about his background instead of being so trusting. But what about the people who knew him before I did and knew what really happened with his first wife? Why didn't they come forward and say, "Do you know what he did?" Nothing like that ever came up, which is why I did not question what he told me. I was shunned for that, and I will probably still be shunned for that.

THE MONSTER WHO KILLED HIS FAMILY TWICE

I know now that there were a lot of warning signs and that I missed them. There were many days I chalked his moods up to the fact that he was having a bad day when those were really red flags. I didn't know at the time. When I was growing up, no one ever talked to me about men or how a husband was supposed to treat a wife. No one talked to me about bad things that could happen, so I was naïve when it came to that.

I am still learning. When he picked fights for no apparent reason, how he treated the kids and tried to cause division in the household . . . those were more signs. I have read about the different types of narcissists and gaslighting and what they do to make themselves feel good and make others feel bad. That was a lot of what I was going through. There were so many things that I didn't know back then. I just tried to do the best that I knew to do at the time.

Stress, unemployment, and substance abuse can be triggers for domestic violence. I struggled to understand what would trigger him, but in the end, being served with divorce papers is what finally pushed him over the edge. Protective orders, court dates and custody hearings are other triggers that can make people really dangerous.

If you are in a relationship and you see red flags or signs of abuse, go the other way—run. It may not be as detrimental as what happened to me, but you never know. He didn't physically abuse me at first, but there was mental and verbal torment. Who wants to go through that, never knowing if today is going to be a good day or a bad day?

Oftentimes when we are in relationships where there is mental or verbal torment we get used to the abuser's abnormal behaviors when we really shouldn't—I know that's what happened to me. We need to realize that we only have one life. We have to love ourselves just how we love our kids. We have to walk away from it.

If you are staying in a situation because you think the person has changed or will change, you have to come to grips with reality. You must accept the relationship for what it is. Some women do not want to do that. They are not ready to face it. But you need to step up and get over your fear and start over. You have to get out of the situation and do something else. It might be hard if you have been with someone for a long time, because of that attachment. But it is never too late to start over, especially when you have kids. You have to think about them first because they are suffering the same way that you are suffering. Even if the abuse is not directed at the kids, they still hear and see what you are going through. Do you really want to put your kids through that?

Women have more rights than they used to, but we're still not there yet. I learned it is not uncommon for a woman to try to get a PPO but she can't. That needs to change. We are not saying enough about this. The system let me down and it should be held accountable. When a woman is in crisis, she needs to be taken seriously. If a judge is going to deny you a PPO, at a minimum they should tell you what steps you need to take instead of saying, "There's nothing we can do to help you." When that happens, you just feel lost. You don't know what to do next and you feel hopeless.

Today I know that there are advocates that can help you file for a PPO, but at the time I had no idea. I did not know who to reach out to or where to get help. No one around me was knowledgeable about it either.

I would like there to be a law in place where women can get more help when they need it. There are some programs out there, and there are some shelters, but there are not enough. There are plenty of statistics and research available to support this truth.

We need to have more resources available, and we need to educate women on what those resources are. Women need to know, "If this is going on, speak to an advocate," and we need to know where those advocates are located so we can reach out to them and get the help we need.

What do you do without a life that you carried within you and helped bring into this world—or in my case, four lives? A lot of people do not understand unless they have had children themselves. It's not like when your kids go off to college. I feel like someone gutted me because they wanted a kid so badly and they left me there to die. That's how the pain is for me.

There are many people that deal with situations involving formerly incarcerated individuals, it just hasn't come out in such a public way like mine has. People have someone in their life who has been to prison; they know people that have murdered and people who are pedophiles or whatever the case may be. Learn from my experience. We can't just put our faith in other people. If I knew from the beginning what he had done, I would not have given him another thought.

EPILOGUE

September 21 is still a hard day for me. I don't like that day. But now I reach out more to my friends instead of just keeping to myself and trying to get through it. It is in your darkest moments when you don't know what to do and you do not reach out that bad things happen or you do bad things to yourself. I have never reached that point, but I do not want to take that risk, so I reach out more often instead of staying to myself or drinking.

Sometimes it is the thinking about the anniversary date ahead of time that makes it worse. The birthdays are hard, especially when they are back-to-back like Chadney's, Kaleigh's, and Koi's are. I used to worry about how I would do on my kids' birthdays but in time I realized all I can do is take it one day at a time and approach those days when they come.

I was in a weird place when my son's birthday came one year, and I felt like I didn't need to be alone. I called one of my friends and left her a voicemail that said, "I just need you to stay on the phone with me. I don't want to be by myself." I was on my way home when she called me back and asked me where I was. She had a spare key to my house, and she was already there waiting for me. I thanked God for that.

I have a lot of memories of my kids, and I had a lot of fun with them. There were times when they made me upset, but I never stayed mad. We would talk about it and then we would be done with it. Kara did not do half of what I tried to get away with as a teenager. I had some really good kids.

My son was an artist. He was creative at an early age, and he was good at putting things together. One of his favorite things to do was play paintball and he also liked airsoft. Chadney was always concerned about me; he was my protector. Sometimes we would do silly things around the house. He liked to hide in a corner and then jump out and scare me. We watched Marvel movies together. He was really funny and a cool kid to hang around with. He was an introvert and kept to himself, but he was starting to come out of his shell more. He had graduated from Specs Howard School of Media Arts and was just starting his own graphic design business.

Kara was creative, too. She was the one who wanted to try everything. She was on the honor roll ever since she started school. She was goal oriented. I never had to tell her to do her homework; she was focused on school and her grades and wanted to be an OB-GYN. She was into cheerleading and track and helped tutor kids. She was making plans for prom and was about to enroll in a medical program—something I did not find out about until after the tragedy. Kara was a caring person, and she loved her family a lot.

Koi had just started first grade. We had moved her to

THE MONSTER WHO KILLED HIS FAMILY TWICE

a private school, and she was liking it. I could see how her mindset was changing. She had overheard some Arab women speaking one day and asked me why they were talking differently. I said, "That's their culture. It's good to learn more than one language because it will help you talk to your friends and it will help you later in life." After that, she wanted to learn a language so I enrolled her in a Spanish class. She adored her big sister and wanted to be just like Kara. Koi was funny and we would always have to tell her, "Push your glasses up." We would tell her she looked like a little old church lady because she liked her dresses and wanted to wear tights. She did not care if it was ninety degrees outside, she wanted to wear tights and dresses all the time.

Kaleigh liked carrying her little purse. First it was Kara's purse and then it was Koi's before Kaleigh had it. Kaleigh would put her hand sanitizer and her lip gloss inside it and carry that purse with her faithfully. She liked makeup and would always play with my eyeshadow. She loved being outside at the park; she could stay outside day and night. She was the youngest, so she was the one that would cling to me. If I turned around, she would be right there. She was lovable and funny in her own way, and I just miss it.

My kids were all in different stages of life and they did not get the chance to fully blossom. That is what hurts—not being able to see their personalities develop and see who they would have become. I miss my kids. I want to touch

THE MONSTER WHO KILLED HIS FAMILY TWICE

them. I want to feel them.

Part of my story includes a horrific tragedy that I will have to deal with every day for the rest of my life. But it is also a story of hope and faith. Hope for people who have been through or are experiencing domestic violence—hope that your situation can get better. Faith that you can overcome whatever situation you are in. You may have to dig deep within to find that faith, but it is worth the effort.

I am not saying it will be easy. That's why it is so important to have a good support system or at least someone to support you. I probably would not have made it without the support of my friends. They are the ones who have really been there for me. I tell them all the time that I love them. I know I was all over the place those first few years after the tragedy and I was not myself. I did a lot of things back then that were questionable. My friends who are closest to me know how I normally am, and they know my kids were my life.

My friends did not always agree with me, but they were still there to support me. It was when people distanced themselves or treated me differently that hurt. My friends have never done that. They have stayed with me through the ups and the downs. When I started drinking too much and was on so many medications, they would tell me the truth about how I was acting. They knew why I was doing it even when I didn't. But they stuck and they stayed there with me through it all.

The trauma that people in domestic violence situations

survive is a hard thing to wrap your mind around. At first, you don't know what you're going to do or how you're going to react. You get severely depressed, and people don't know what you are going through. How could they? That's why I thank God for my close friends who have been with me the entire time. They may not understand all of it, but they love me and accept me for who I am. They never left me. They are my family.

I am in a good place today. This is the most peace I have felt since my kids passed and I stay away from anyone or anything that threatens that. I know now that when I feel a certain way I need to talk about it with someone and get my feelings out. Substance abuse is not the solution. It did not get me anywhere and it won't get you anywhere either. People can get stuck there and lose ten, fifteen, twenty years. I did not want that to be me. Find that faith in yourself and push through. Because even when you are out of the abusive situation, sometimes you still feel hopeless. Reach out and talk to someone. That is what has helped me the most.

The night we were tied up in the basement, my husband said I was going to suffer. I thought to myself, *No, I'm not going to suffer,* but I did not realize until later what he meant. He took my kids, and they were the most important beings to me. He shot me in the foot and tried to cripple me and he cut my face and tried to disfigure me. I have had some surgeries on my face because I was in a lot of pain, but I've never had any plastic surgery. My scar doesn't bother me, and it does not make me an ugly person. I am still a beautiful woman.

My strength today comes from that moment in the basement, and it comes from thinking about my kids. I know they would not want me to be sad. They would want me to be happy so I have to think about that a lot even though it is bittersweet because I want my kids and I can't have them. But there is still life after exhausting, evil things happen to us. I am living proof. I will not suffer. I am not broken.

THE MONSTER WHO KILLED HIS FAMILY TWICE

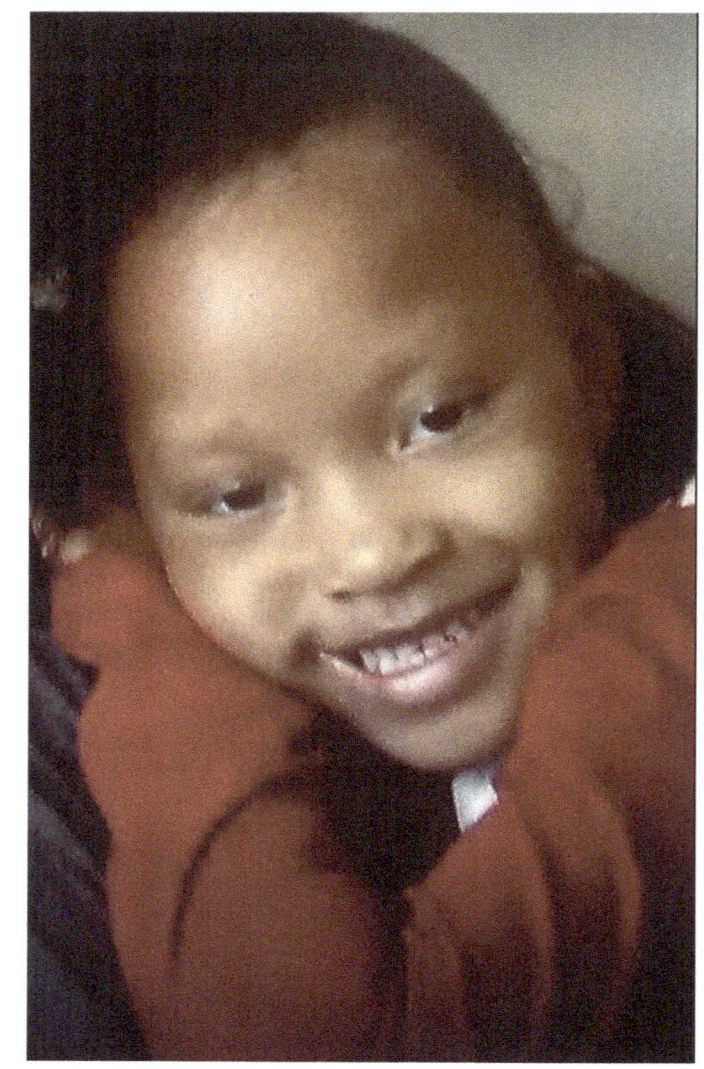

THE MONSTER WHO KILLED HIS FAMILY TWICE

THE MONSTER WHO KILLED HIS FAMILY TWICE

THE MONSTER WHO KILLED HIS FAMILY TWICE

THE MONSTER WHO KILLED HIS FAMILY TWICE

THE MONSTER WHO KILLED HIS FAMILY TWICE

THE MONSTER WHO KILLED HIS FAMILY TWICE

THE MONSTER WHO KILLED HIS FAMILY TWICE

THE MONSTER WHO KILLED HIS FAMILY TWICE

THE MONSTER WHO KILLED HIS FAMILY TWICE

THE MONSTER WHO KILLED HIS FAMILY TWICE

THE MONSTER WHO KILLED HIS FAMILY TWICE

THE MONSTER WHO KILLED HIS FAMILY TWICE

THE MONSTER WHO KILLED HIS FAMILY TWICE

THE MONSTER WHO KILLED HIS FAMILY TWICE

THE MONSTER WHO KILLED HIS FAMILY TWICE

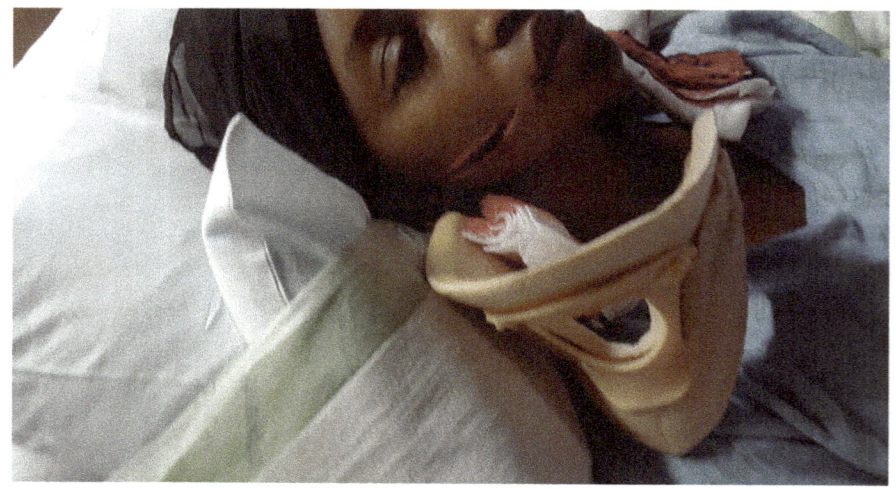

THE MONSTER WHO KILLED HIS FAMILY TWICE

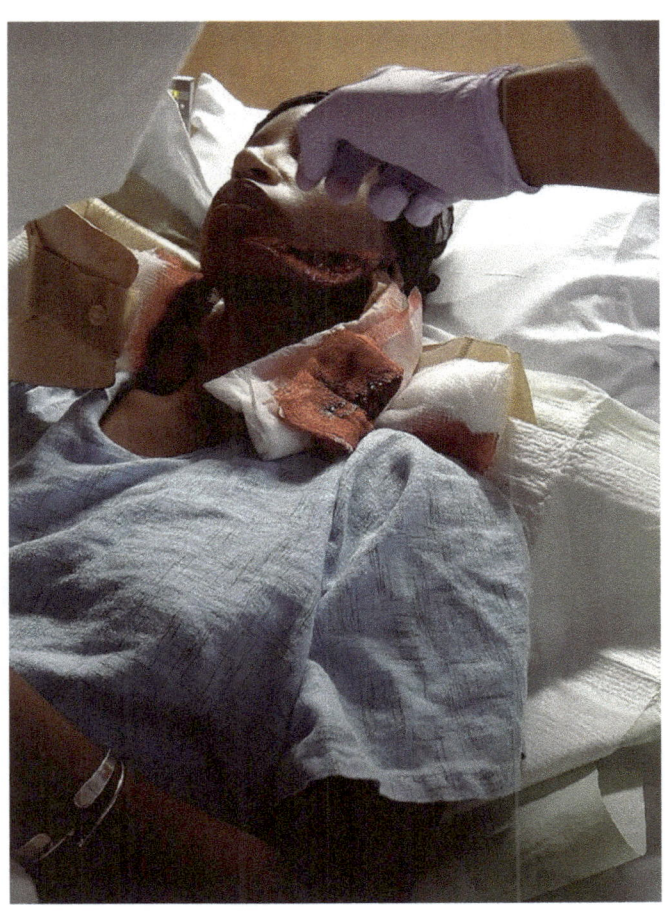

THE MONSTER WHO KILLED HIS FAMILY TWICE

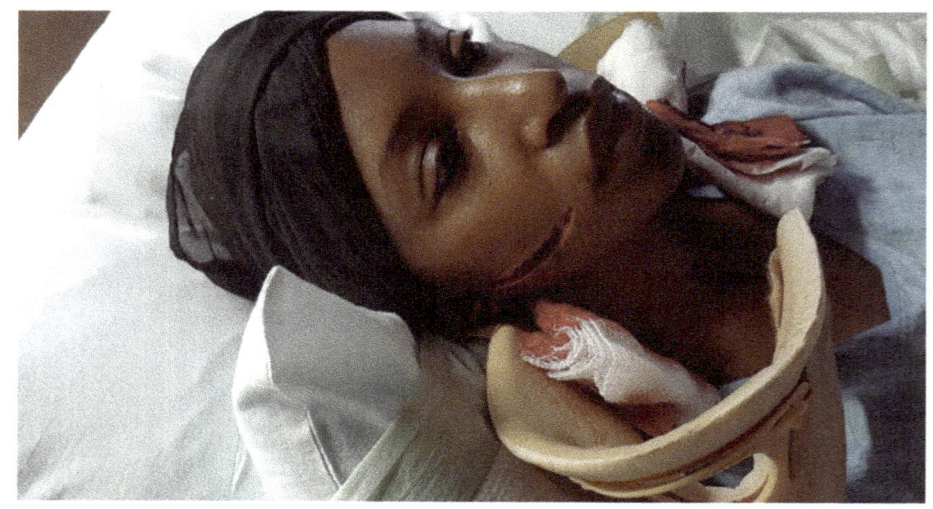

THE MONSTER WHO KILLED HIS FAMILY TWICE

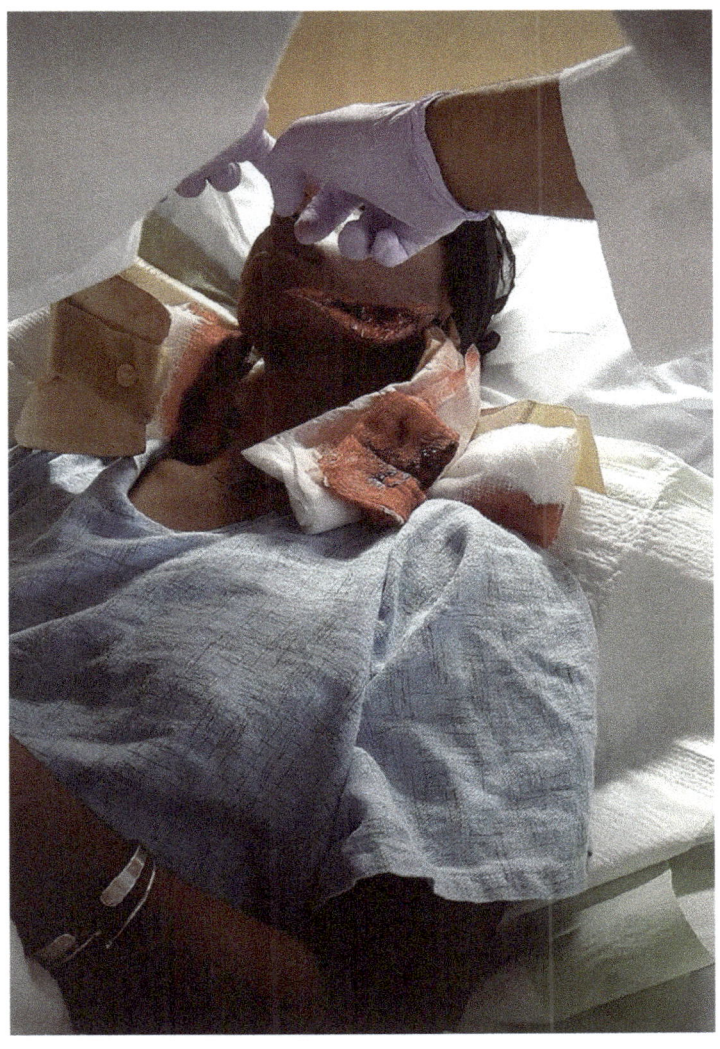

THE MONSTER WHO KILLED HIS FAMILY TWICE

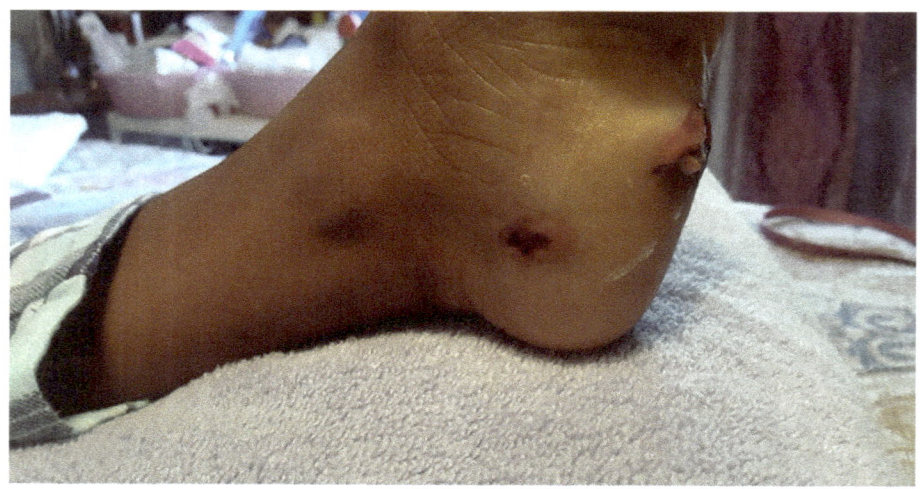

THE MONSTER WHO KILLED HIS FAMILY TWICE

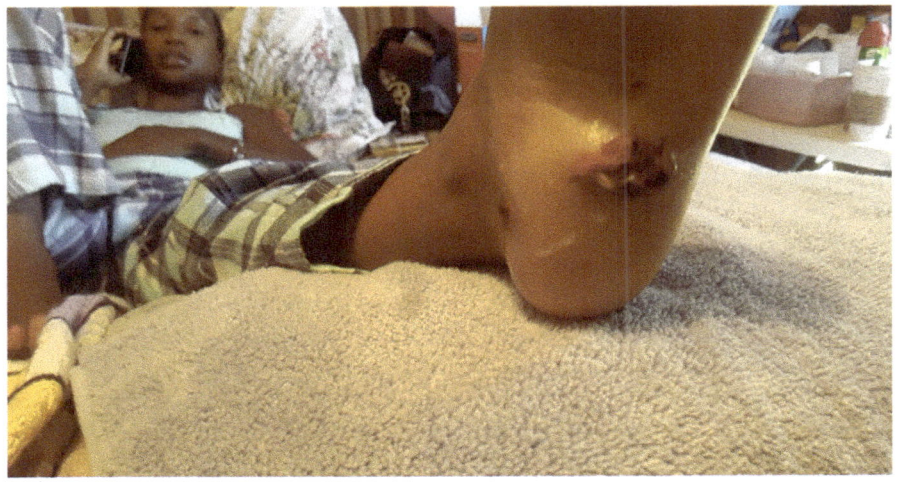

THE MONSTER WHO KILLED HIS FAMILY TWICE

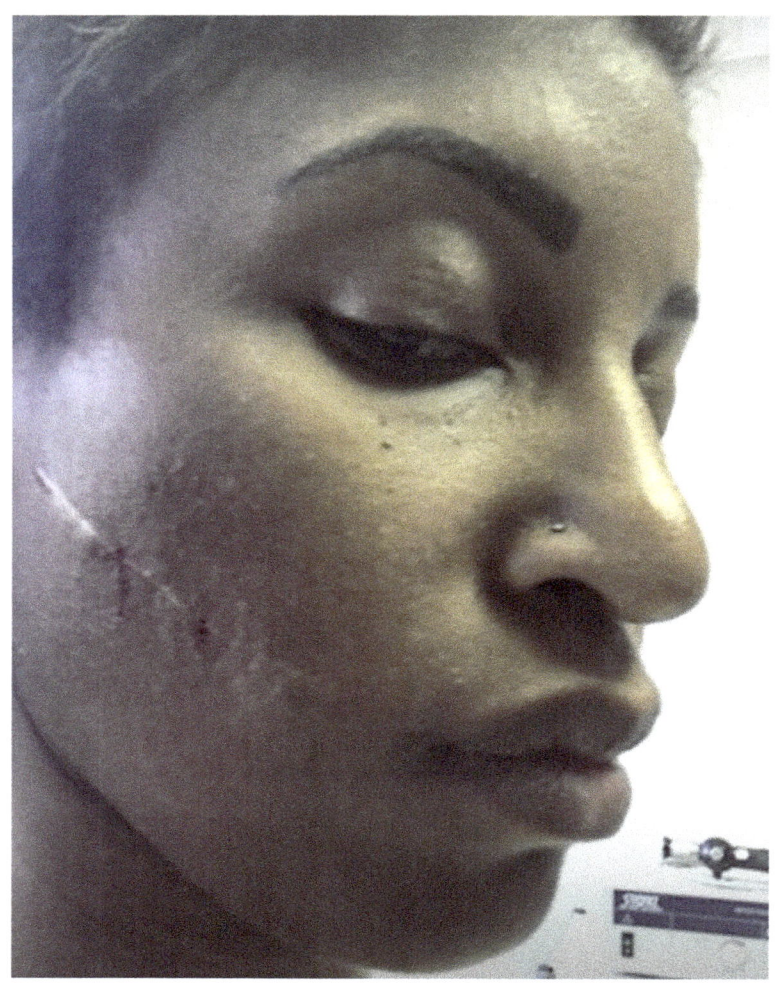

THE MONSTER WHO KILLED HIS FAMILY TWICE

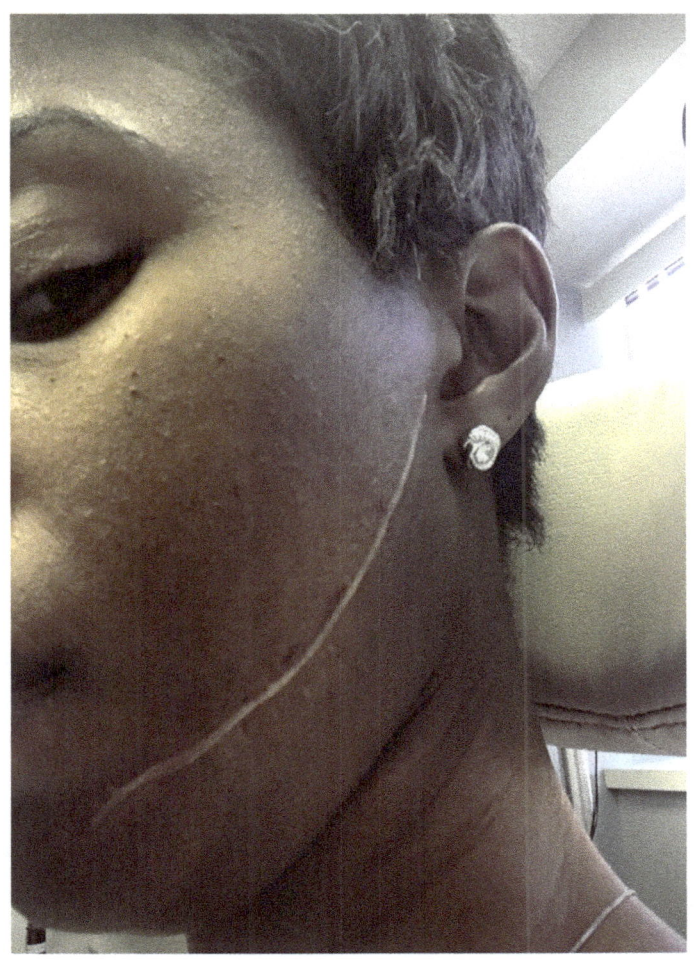

THE MONSTER WHO KILLED HIS FAMILY TWICE

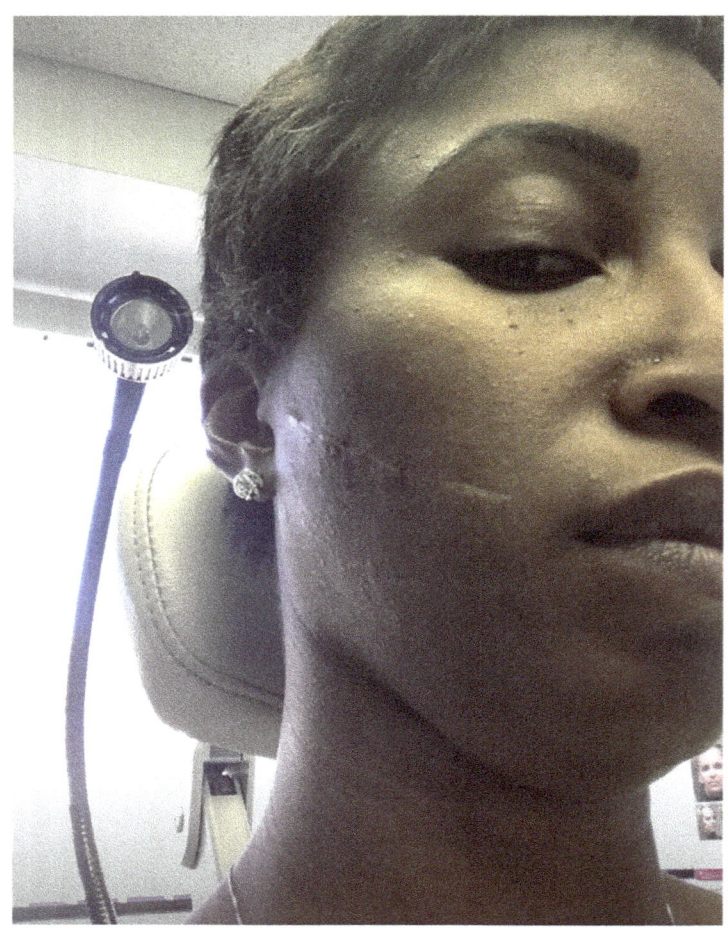

RESOURCES

For a list of local resources in your area, search the directory of assistance providers on the National Domestic Violence Hotline website or view a list by state on the Office on Women's Health website. Each of the organizations listed below provides even more information and resources so you or your loved one can safely get help.

If you are thinking about leaving, prepare a safety plan in advance so you and your children can protect yourselves. These resources will help you do that.

Battered Women's Justice Project
bwjp.org
800.903.0111 ext. 1

FaithTrust Institute
faithtrustinstitute.org
206.634.1903

First Step
Firststep-mi.org
24-hour Help Line: 734.722.6800

National Coalition Against Domestic Violence
ncadv.org
303.839.1852

National Domestic Violence Hotline
thehotline.org
800.799.7233
Text "START" to 88788

National Network to End Domestic Violence
nnedv.org
202.543.5566

Office on Women's Health
(for resources by state)
Womenshealth.gov
800.994.9662

Story Terrace

www.ingramcontent.com/pod-product-compliance
Lightning Source LLC
LaVergne TN
LVHW061531070526
838199LV00010B/451